MASTERING THE
INSTANT VORTEX PLUS

A Practical Guide to the 7-in-1 Air Fryer and All Its Functions

T0073015

JAMES O. FRAIOLI

Good Books®

New York, New York

Good Books books may be purchased in bulk at special discounts for sales
promotion, corporate gifts, fund-raising, or educational purposes. Special
editions can also be created to specifications. For details, contact the Special
Sales Department, Good Books, 307 West 36th Street, 11th Floor, New York,
NY 10018 or info@skyhorsepublishing.com.

Good Books is an imprint of Skyhorse Publishing, Inc.®, a Delaware
corporation.

Visit our website at www.goodbooks.com

10 9 8 7 6 5 4 3 2

Library of Congress Cataloging-in-Publication Data is available on file.

Cover design by Daniel Brount
Cover photograph by Tucker + Hossler

Print ISBN: 978-1-5107-5846-9
Ebook ISBN: 978-1-5107-5848-3

Printed in the United States of America

CONTENTS

INTRODUCTION

A mericans are hungrier than ever for home-cooked meals.

According to the market research firm NPD Group, four out of five meals in the United States are prepared at home. It's no surprise that kitchen countertop appliances like one-pot cookers and air fryers continue to sweep the nation. Now, the makers of the Instant Pot, America's number one bestselling small kitchen appliance, introduce home cooks to the Instant Vortex Plus Air Fryer Oven.

Designed to support an active lifestyle and those who want to cook healthy and fast, the Instant Vortex Plus Air Fryer Oven is a compact ten-quart capacity air fryer with an advanced microprocessor and seven Smart Programs.

Whether you prefer cooking with fresh or frozen ingredients, the Instant Vortex Plus Air Fryer Oven uses One-Step Even-Crisp Technology and 1,500 watts of power so you can cook anything and everything to your liking. Air frying, broiling, toasting, baking, roasting, reheating, dehydrating, and preparing food rotisserie style. You can do it all with just one appliance. And one of the best features of the Instant Vortex Plus Air Fryer Oven is its ability to use circulating superheated air to cook the food and still be able to achieve that crunchy golden deep-fried flavor with up to 95 percent less oil than traditional deep fryers. That's a nice healthy alternative.

Think of air fryers like the Instant Vortex Plus Air Fryer Oven as small convection ovens. This means they have a heating element along with a motorized fan that circulates hot air inside a cooking chamber. Because air fryers use a higher speed to circulate the hot air, foods are able to cook evenly while creating that same crispiness and crunch that many find in traditional fried foods, such as French fries or chicken wings, but without the oil. In addition, because the cooking chamber is smaller than a conventional oven, the hot, high-speed, circulating air is confined to a much smaller space. This reduces cooking times by 20 percent or more when compared to traditional cooking methods. Recipes that say foods need to be heated for ten minutes may only require six minutes in an air fryer.

Remember, air fryers aren't frying the food. The hot, high-speed circulating air is.

The air also removes some of the moisture from the food, and that's a good thing, resulting in the same characteristics as fried foods, but with significantly lower fat levels because there isn't any oil being used. In addition, when it is air fried, food experiences a chemical reaction known as the Maillard reaction, in which the food browns in color and becomes more flavorful, just like it does from other cooking methods.

From small college dorms to large city apartments, the Instant Vortex Plus Air Fryer Oven is fast, versatile, and convenient, perfect for both couples and small families who appreciate a variety of cooking methods but who have limited space.

Should you invest in an Instant Vortex Plus Air Fryer Oven, if you haven't already?

For beginning cooks, or those who enjoy spending time in the kitchen, the Instant Vortex Plus Air Fryer Oven is relatively inexpensive and offers seven different cooking methods with which to experiment: air fry, broil, bake, roast, reheat, dehydrate, and rotisserie. Knowing what temperatures and cooking times go with each Smart Program will take time along with some trial and error, but if you're invested in the appliance, the learning process will pay off with delicious, healthier meals that are cooked quickly at home.

In this book, we will begin by opening up the Instant Vortex Plus Air Fryer Oven box and setting up the appliance for immediate use.

You'll quickly come to realize that this innovative kitchen appliance is cute and sleek and will fit perfectly on your kitchen countertop without taking up much space. Some online bloggers find the Instant Vortex Plus Air Fryer

Oven to be a bit larger than comparable air fryers. However, given its wide range of features, the rotisserie option in particular, the size is understandable.

The chapters ahead will look at the seven Smart Programs that are built inside the Instant Vortex Plus Air Fryer Oven.

These programs will allow you to air fry, broil, toast, bake, roast, reheat, dehydrate, and cook rotisserie style all in one oven. The Instant Vortex Plus Air Fryer Oven is also very convenient because of its quick cooking and little to no preheating time. In addition, and unlike other countertop appliances like the Instant Pot, Ninja Foodi, and other air fryers, the Instant Vortex Plus Air Fryer Oven has a glass air fryer door so you can watch your food cook. There's even an interior light to help you see the cooking chamber inside.

Last, we will discuss proper cleaning of and care for your Instant Vortex Plus Air Fryer Oven, and look at some of the safety precautions.

If you're ready to open the box that contains the Instant Vortex Plus Air Fryer Oven, turn the pages ahead and begin your gastronomic journey into the world of air frying—Instant Vortex style.

FIRST-TIMERS USING THE INSTANT VORTEX PLUS

Getting Familiar with the Appliance

INITIAL SETUP

Opening the product box containing the ten-quart Instant Vortex Plus Air Fryer Oven, you will soon find that the appliance is much smaller than the manufacturer's box, so don't let the large packaging intimidate you.

When you lift the cardboard lid, the first items you should find are the **rotisserie fetch** and the **rotisserie spit and forks** (three included accessories). Remove these items from the Styrofoam packaging and set them aside.

Also, remove the **Instant Vortex Plus Air Fryer Oven Safety, Maintenance & Warranty Booklet,** and **Getting Started Guide** and set them aside.

Next, remove the Styrofoam top, which will allow you access to the relatively lightweight **Instant Vortex Plus Air Fryer Oven**. Carefully lift the oven out of the box and set the appliance on a stable, level counter, table, or surface, away from combustible material and external heat sources. Leave at least five inches around the oven. Remove the protective layer covering the unit. Make sure not to place anything on top of the oven and do not block the air vent in the back of the appliance.

Remove the plastic wrapper covering the power cord and the two pieces of tape on each side of the stainless steel oven face. Now, carefully open the glass air fryer door while removing the "Caution" slip.

With the glass air fryer door open, slide out and remove the cardboard sleeve, then slide out the **rotisserie basket** with the attached Styrofoam protectors. Remove the protectors, along with the two small Styrofoam squares, and set the rotisserie basket aside.

Carefully slide out the two **cooking trays** and **drip pan** wrapped in plastic. Remove the plastic and set the trays aside.

You now have the following components:

- Ten-quart Instant Vortex Plus Air Fryer Oven (approximately 14" x 13" x 9-¼")
- Rotisserie fetch
- Rotisserie spit and forks
- Rotisserie basket
- Two cooking trays
- Drip pan

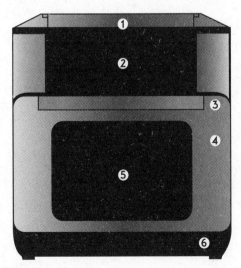

1: AIR VENTS (REAR)

2: CONTROL PANEL

3: HEATING ELEMENT (INTERIOR)

4: OVEN DOOR

5: COOKING CHAMBER (INTERIOR)

6: POWER CORD (REAR)

ADDITIONAL ACCESSORIES

Before we move further along, let's quickly look at a helpful list of suggested accessories that do not come with the Instant Vortex Plus Air Fryer Oven but are items you should have on hand, especially if you're planning to cook often with the appliance:

Aluminum foil: Great for wrapping the cooking trays and drip pan to keep your cleaning to a minimum.

Baking pans: Small, inexpensive baking and pizza pans by Crofton and Pampered Chef slide easily into the Instant Vortex Plus Air Fryer Oven, some easily replacing the cooking tray, while allowing for good airflow. The Crofton pizza pan, for example, fits nicely in the cooking chamber but will need to sit on the cooking tray.

Cookares springform set: Get the eight-inch set, with Bundt pan. This accessory fits perfectly on the cooking tray and is ideal when you are baking with the Instant Vortex Plus Air Fryer Oven.

Foil mini loaf pans: These disposable pans are inexpensive and handy.

Glass baking dishes/bowls: A 1.5-quart glass or eight-inch oven-safe dish or bowl will fit comfortably on top of the cooking tray and inside the Instant Vortex Plus Air Fryer Oven. If there are handles on the side of the dish/bowl, slide the vessel into the oven at a diagonal.

Individual silicone baking cups: These are very inexpensive, colorful, and versatile. You can get nine on each cooking tray, eighteen total, so use these if you're planning to make a lot of muffins.

Muffin trays: Whether you use a minimuffin tray, a standard four-count muffin tray, or a deep silicone muffin tray, they will work well in your Instant Vortex Plus Air Fryer Oven without compromising airflow. To add additional room, simply flip over the cooking tray in the cooking chamber and set the muffin tray on top. Due to the small size of the cooking chamber, only one muffin tray will fit at one time.

Oven mitts: Always important when handling hot foods and appliances. Try a pair of silicone-insulated lined mitts. They allow your hands more flexibility and grip while keeping them safe from hot temperatures.

Pyrex oven-safe loaf pan (4¾ Cup): This glass casserole pan is small and versatile and works well with the Instant Vortex Plus Air Fryer Oven. Make sure the pan is suitable for oven temperatures of 400°F (the highest temperature of the Instant Vortex Plus Air Fryer Oven).

Silicone mat: Place over the air fryer door so your food doesn't spill onto the glass when inserting and removing from the Instant Vortex Plus Air Fryer Oven chamber.

Small porcelain ramekins: Ramekins are small and durable, and you can get four ramekins on each cooking tray while maintaining good airflow. From cheesecake to mac 'n' cheese, these are excellent to use when cooking with the Instant Vortex Plus Air Fryer Oven.

THE CONTROLS

You have unpacked the Instant Vortex Plus Air Fryer Oven and have familiarized yourself with what comes with the appliance and what additional accessories you should have on hand. Next, it's time to study the digital control panel of the Instant Vortex Plus Air Fryer Oven. This is where all the functions are located.

LED display: This large digital display shows cooking temperature, time, reminders, and error messages.

Smart Program panel: Includes AirFry, Roast, Broil, Bake, Reheat, and Dehydrate. Each Smart Program includes a default cooking temperature and time. Simply select a Smart Program from the panel on the touchscreen to begin.

> **AirFry:** For chicken, chicken wings, French fries, and more, this is the function to use. You'll need very little oil, if any, and you'll enjoy wonderful grease-free results.
>
> **Roast:** Whether it's a whole chicken or a beef roast, you'll achieve a savory cooked center-piece to your meal in less time. Two cooking

trays give you room for roasted veggies and other sides, too.

Broil: Perfect top-heavy heat for braising your favorite dishes evenly, from salmon to steak. You can also melt cheese for toast, nachos, or on top of soups or potatoes. This is also the function you will use when you want to **Toast** something.

Bake: From cakes to muffins to baked potatoes, even baking temperatures means fantastic baked items each time.

Reheat: Start up your Instant Vortex Plus Air Fryer Oven for a quick warm-up. Better than a microwave, it will allow you to reheat your food without drying it out or making it soft and chewy.

Dehydrate: Beef jerky, dried fruit, and veggie chips are just several snacks you can make using the Dehydrate function. Enjoy preservative-free snacks with plenty of nutritional value from the comfort of your own kitchen.

Rotisserie: A whole chicken or beef roast turns out perfectly with this rotisserie-style feature.

Adjusting temperature: Located on the left side of the LED display. To adjust the cooking temperature, press the +/- sign and hold to quickly adjust.

Adjusting time: Located on the right side of the LED display. To adjust the cooking time, press the +/- sign and hold to quickly adjust.

Start: Touch the Start key to begin cooking.

ADDITIONAL CONTROLS

Rotate: When cooking has begun, touch this button to turn the rotisserie rotation on or off.

Light: Touch this button to turn the internal chamber light on and off. The light automatically turns off after two minutes.

Cancel: Touch this button to cancel cooking. The oven will return to the Standby mode while displaying the word OFF.

Sound on/off: Touch and hold both (–) keys (Temp and Time) for three seconds to turn the sound on or off. However, error alerts cannot be silenced.

Smart Program reset: When in Standby mode, touch and hold the Smart Program you would like to reset for three seconds. The Smart Program cooking time and temperature will be restored to the default setting.

Full reset: When in Standby mode, touch and hold both the Temp and Time plus (+) signs at the same time for three seconds. All the Smart Programs cooking times and temperatures will be restored to the default settings.

1. DISPLAY
2. SMART PROGRAMS
3. TEMPERATURE
4. TIME
5. START
6. ROTATE ON/OFF
7. LIGHT ON/OFF
8. CANCEL

TEST RUN

Now that you're familiar with the digital control panel and have all the Instant Vortex Plus Air Fryer Oven components in front of you, let's test the appliance before you cook.

With the glass air fryer door open, place the drip pan on the bottom of the cooking chamber. This pan is made from aluminum coated with Teflon, which makes for easy cleanup. Next, connect the power cord and three-prong grounded plug to a 120V power source. To reduce the risk of electrical shock, plug into a grounded electrical outlet that is easily accessible. As soon as the oven is plugged in, you should hear a short beep followed by the word OFF illuminated in the LED display. This means the oven is in Standby mode.

Note: To unplug the oven, grasp the plug and pull slowly from the outlet. Never pull from the power cord.

Now, select one of the six Smart Programs: AirFry, Roast, Broil, Bake, Reheat, and Dehydrate.

For our test, let's select AirFry by lightly touching the button on the intuitive touchscreen. You will hear a short beep. The cooking temperature on the display should read 400°F.

Use the +/- Time keys to change the cooking time from the manufacture preset time of eighteen minutes to twenty minutes. Each increment of temperature will change with a short beep.

Note: The Smart Program will automatically save your last temperature and time settings. As noted in the Controls section, to reset the Smart Program back to the default settings, simply touch and hold the Smart Program for three seconds. To reset all the Smart Programs back to the default settings, touch and hold both + keys (Temp and Time) for three seconds.

Next, touch the green START button to begin heating. You should hear a beep and then hear the subtle fan kick on to warm the oven. When the oven reaches the designated temperature you programmed, the display will alert you to "Add Food," accompanied by a series of beeps.

For our test, do not add any food to the cooking chamber. However, when you cook with the appliance later, you can add food before or after preheating the unit.

Open the glass air fryer door (the fan will pause) and carefully insert the cooking trays into the hot cooking chamber.

Close the glass air fryer door (the fan will reengage) while the display will remind you of the current temperature setting while counting down your preselected time.

During the Smart Program operation, the oven will emit a series of beeps alerting you to "Turn Food," which will also be visible on the digital display. When cooking with both cooking trays, make sure to swap their positions in the cooking chamber when you are notified to "Turn Food."

Open the glass air fryer door to automatically pause the Smart Program and close the glass air fryer door to resume.

Note: The notice to "Turn Food" will only appear during the AirFry and Roast settings. Cooking will then proceed after ten seconds, whether the food has been turned or not. If "Rotate" is turned on, the message will not appear.

When there is only one minute of cooking time remaining, the cook time counts down in seconds. On all Smart Programs, except

Dehydrate, the word "Cool" is displayed, accompanied by a series of beeps when the countdown is finished, followed by the fan being activated to cool the oven.

Note: The oven will still be hot after the "Cool" cycle. Always make sure not to touch any hot surfaces and always use oven mitts to remove the cooking trays from the cooking chamber.

When the Smart Program is finished, the word End will illuminate on the display, accompanied by a series of beeps.

Make sure to allow the oven to cool to room temperature before removing and cleaning the accessories and cooking chamber. Since we didn't cook anything this time, there won't be anything to clean.

For proper care and cleaning instructions, please refer to pages 111–113.

How are you feeling with the Instant Vortex Plus Air Fryer Oven so far? Confident? If you are, let's start cooking!

FUNCTION 1

AIR FRYER

Of the seven Instant Vortex Plus Air Fryer Oven functions, the AirFry function will probably be the one you use most frequently. This is because there are many delicious foods you can air fry. As we discussed in the Introduction, the air fryer replaces hot oil with superheated circulating air to produce fabulous deep-fried-style foods, but without any of the oil. And that's a good thing. The AirFry function seals the food's juiciness on the inside while coating the outside with that crisp, crunchy, browned texture we're accustomed to enjoying with deep frying. The result is air-fried foods that are quicker and easier to make, and cleaner and healthier for you to eat.

Because the fan and heating element of the Instant Vortex Plus Air Fryer Oven are situated at the top of the appliance, you may be instructed to turn or rotate your food for even air frying. To rotate the food, simply swap the top cooking rack with the bottom cooking rack.

Let's begin by walking through the general steps for how to use the AirFry function. We'll then look at several examples, including how to air fry bacon, hamburgers, and French fries, so you can better understand the simplicity of the AirFry feature.

To begin:

1. Select the AirFry function from the Control Panel display.
2. Select the temperature. The temperature will default to 400°F. To increase or decrease the temperature, press the up (+) and down (-) arrows from the Temp function located on the left side of the appliance.

3. Select the cooking time. To increase or decrease the cooking time, press the up (+) and down (-) arrows from the Time function located on the right side of the appliance.

4. If using the rotisserie basket to air fry, you will need to press the Rotate button at this time.

5. Press Start to begin. The digital display will illuminate the word ON.

6. Prepare your ingredients.

7. When the Instant Vortex Plus Air Fryer Oven reaches temperature, the digital display will alert you to "Add Food," accompanied by a series of beeps. When using accessories like the rotisserie basket, you may ignore the "Add Food" prompt, as the food will already be inside the basket and cooking.

8. Add the food, making sure the drip pan is securely in place. The great advantage of the Instant Vortex Plus Air Fryer Oven, unlike other air fryers, is that the appliance comes with two cooking trays

and a rotisserie, allowing you to cook a lot more food than a standard air fryer.

9. Close the glass air fryer door to begin cooking.

10. Rather than stopping or opening up a lid to check on your food, the Instant Vortex Plus Air Fryer Oven will automatically alert you to "Turn Food." At this time, turn the food and/or rotate the cooking trays for even cooking. Not all food needs turning or rotating, as when you're using the rotisserie basket, so this alert depends on what specifically you are air frying. If you do not need to turn the food, no problem. Cooking will proceed after ten seconds, whether the food has been turned or not.

11. Close the glass air fryer door to resume cooking.

12. When there is only one minute of cooking time remaining, the cook time will count down in seconds. When no time is left, the word COOL will be displayed, accompanied by a series of beeps, followed by the fan being activated to cool the oven.

13. When the Instant Vortex Plus Air Fryer Oven is finished cooling, the word END will illuminate on the display, accompanied by another series of beeps.

14. Wearing your oven mitts, carefully open the glass air fryer door and remove the food and trays from the cooking chamber. Use caution, because the door and accessories will be hot. If using the rotisserie basket, you will need to use both your oven mitts and the rotisserie fetch tool to remove the basket.

Air Frying Tip: Sometimes when you're cooking with multiple cooking trays, the food on the top tray will crisp more than the food on the bottom tray. For example, if you're cooking chicken wings, you may find the wings on the top tray are crispier than the wings on the bottom tray. This may be a result of the chicken drippings falling through the perforated holes on the top cooking tray and "moistening" the wings on the bottom cooking tray. To solve this, cook in batches. Remove the wings that are crispy and replace the less-crispy wings from the bottom cooking tray to the top cooking tray, so all the wings are equally cooked and crispy.

AirFry Examples:

Air Frying Bacon Using the Cooking Trays

Bacon is one of those delicious ingredients we like to cook, but it often comes with its fair share of splatter and mess. Not so in the Instant Vortex Plus Air Fryer Oven.

To begin, make sure the drip pan is securely in place. Press the AirFry button from the Control Panel display, set the temperature to 375°F, and set the time to seven to nine minutes, depending on how crispy you like your bacon and how thick the bacon is. Then press the Start button. The Instant Vortex Plus Air Fryer Oven will then display the word ON. Do not add the bacon just yet. Allow the oven to preheat, which will take about two or three minutes—a lot less time than with your convection oven.

While the Instant Vortex Plus Air Fryer Oven is preheating, now is a good time to prepare the bacon. Simply arrange the desired amount of bacon strips on the cooking trays (do not overlap the strips), about four or five strips per cooking tray (eight to ten strips total) if the bacon is placed horizontally.

When the Instant Vortex Plus Air Fryer Oven says to "Add Food," and the timer goes off, open the glass air fryer door (you don't have to press or cancel anything), slide the cooking trays with the bacon inside the oven (middle rack for one tray; top and middle rack for two trays), and close the door. The Instant Vortex Plus Air Fryer Oven will automatically start and count down the minutes. The glass air fryer door also makes it very convenient to see your food being cooked. If needed, press the Light button to illuminate the inside of the oven.

At the halfway mark, the Instant Vortex Plus Air Fryer Oven will automatically alert you to "Turn Food." Only do so if you're cooking with two cooking trays. Simply swap the top tray with the bottom try. If cooking with one tray, you can ignore the alert, as the cooking will resume.

When the cooking is complete, the Instant Vortex Plus Air Fryer Oven will automatically switch to "Cool" mode and then display the word END.

Wearing oven mitts, open the glass air fryer door and remove the cooking trays from the oven. Use caution, because the door and accessories will be hot.

The bacon should be cooked to perfection.

To add more cooking time if your bacon is not to your liking, simply press the up (+) arrow from the Time function. You can also increase or decrease the cooking temperature while your food is cooking by simply pressing the up (+) and down (-) arrows from the Temp function.

Another good practice after cooking is to keep the glass air fryer door open if children and pets are not in the vicinity. This allows the oven to cool much quicker before cleaning.

Air Frying Hamburgers

Like bacon, hamburgers are another popular food you'll find yourself cooking often with the Instant Vortex Plus Air Fryer Oven. And again, with a lot less splatter and mess.

To begin, let's select a high-quality hamburger meat, preferably 80/20. This ratio means there is

80 percent lean beef to 20 percent fat. You need a little fat in your meat to keep the burgers moist. The extra fat also keeps your burgers from sticking and adds a ton of flavor. Hamburger meat without any fat often results in a very dry, crumbly burger no matter how you cook it. An 80/20 or 70/30 will yield a delicious-tasting burger. Next, form the hamburger meat into 3/4-inch patties while making sure not to overwork the meat with your hands. Overworking will result in a tough burger. Season the patties with some salt and set aside.

To begin, make sure the drip pan is securely in place. Press the AirFry button from the Control Panel display, set the temperature to 375°F, set the time to fifteen minutes, then press the Start button. The Instant Vortex Plus Air Fryer Oven will then display the word ON. Do not add the burgers just yet. Allow the oven to preheat, which will take about two or three minutes, a lot less than your convection oven.

While the Instant Vortex Plus Air Fryer Oven is preheating, now is a good time to arrange those burgers on your cooking trays, making sure not to overlap any of the patties.

When the Instant Vortex Plus Air Fryer Oven says to "Add Food," and the timer goes off, open the glass air fryer door (you don't have to press or cancel anything), slide the cooking trays with the burgers inside the oven, and close the door. The Instant Vortex Plus Air Fryer Oven will automatically start and count down for fifteen minutes. The glass air fryer door also makes it very easy to see your food being cooked. If needed, press the Light button to illuminate the inside of the oven.

When the cooking is complete (no need to flip the burgers), the Instant Vortex Plus Air Fryer Oven will automatically switch to "Cool" mode and then display the word END.

Wearing oven mitts, open the glass air fryer door and remove the cooking trays from the oven. Use caution, because the door and accessories will be hot. The burgers should be cooked to perfection (with an internal temperature of about 160°F).

To add more or less cooking time while your food is cooking, simply press the up (+) and down (-) arrows from the Time function. You can also increase or decrease the cooking temperature while your food is cooking by simply pressing the up (+) and down (-) arrows from the Temp function.

Again, a good kitchen practice after cooking is to keep the glass air fryer door open. This allows the oven to cool much quicker before cleaning.

Air Frying French Fries Using the Rotisserie Basket

Of course, we cannot make hamburgers without having some delicious French fries on the side. After all, who doesn't love French fries? And making crispy fries in the Instant Vortex Plus Air Fryer Oven without having to use a deep fryer or pot of bubbling oil is a huge win for the home cook. Here's how we do it while illustrating the AirFry function and how to properly use the rotisserie basket.

If you'd like to make fresh hand-cut French fries from scratch, simply slice your potatoes (preferably russet) into French fry sticks. Place them in a large bowl and toss with a little vegetable oil.

If you prefer frozen French fries from the freezer section of your grocery store, try the

Ore-Ida Golden Crinkles French Fried Potatoes, if you haven't already. They're made from the highest-quality Grade A potatoes grown in the United States and are perfect for dipping. Another French fry is the Canadian brand Les Fermes Cavendish Farms Flavour Crisp Crispy Straight Cut Classic French Fries. Both of these frozen French fries work extremely well in the Instant Vortex Plus Air Fryer Oven.

Next, place the French fries (fresh or frozen) in the rotisserie basket. Because the basket doesn't stand upright on the counter (due to the prongs mounted at the ends of the basket), find a suitable bowl and set the basket inside the bowl for upright support and balance.

When loading your basket with French fries, make sure you don't overcrowd or overfill the basket, or your fries will steam instead of air frying. The basket should comfortably hold enough French fries from 1½ to 2 potatoes (about 1 pound), depending on the size of your potatoes, or about 20 ounces of frozen French fries. A good measure is to only fill your basket half full with French fries.

Open the glass air frying door. Note: To prevent the oil from the French fries dripping onto the glass door, place a silicone mat (see accessories, page 12) over the door.

Secure the rotisserie basket lid on top by aligning the tab on the rotisserie basket with the notch in the lid. Turn the lid clockwise to "lock" it in place. A "lock-unlock" diagram on top of the lid will help you turn the lid in the proper direction.

Make sure the drip pan is in place on the bottom of the cooking chamber before air frying.

Rotisserie Catch Lever
This is the red lever you see on the left-hand side after you open the glass air fryer door. Moving the lever to the right will allow the rotisserie catch to retract. Look inside the air fryer door, as you move the lever to the right, and you will see a small black knob on the left that moves with the lever. This is the rotisserie catch that creates the space to receive the rotisserie basket.

Securing the Rotisserie Basket
Holding the rotisserie catch lever to the right,

slide the rotisserie basket along the guides in the cooking chamber. Use the rotisserie fetch tool that's included with the Instant Vortex Plus Air Fryer Oven to insert and remove the rotisserie basket after cooking.

Align the ends of the rotisserie basket with the hole in the center of the rotisserie catch, then release the rotisserie catch lever to lock the basket firmly in place. You may have to wiggle the basket a little so the accessory "locks" inside the rotisserie catch. You will hear a locking noise, confirming the rotisserie basket is locked in place. Wiggle the rotisserie basket to make sure it's held firmly in place on both sides of the cooking chamber.

Once the basket is secured in place, remove the silicone mat (if using) and close the glass air fryer door.

When making French fries, you do not need to preheat the Instant Vortex Plus Air Fryer Oven.

To begin, press the AirFry button from the Control Panel display, set the temperature to 400° F, set the time to sixteen minutes, press the Rotate button so the basket will rotate while the French fries air fry, and then press the Start button. The Instant Vortex Plus Air Fryer Oven will then display the word ON as the basket begins to rotate for sixteen minutes.

The rotating function of the Instant Vortex Plus Air Fryer Oven is a convenient feature. Unlike other air fryers or deep fryers, you don't have to stop to lift and shake the basket before resuming cooking. With the basket constantly rotating, the oven tosses the French fries for you, allowing them to air fry and not steam.

When the Instant Vortex Plus Air Fryer Oven beeps and says to "Add Food," simply ignore this message, as your French fries are already cooking.

When the cooking cycle is complete, the Instant Vortex Plus Air Fryer Oven will automatically switch to "Cool" mode and then display the word END.

Wearing your oven mitts, carefully open the glass air fryer door. Use caution, because the door and accessories will be hot. To release the rotisserie basket, insert the rotisserie fetch tool to "hook" the prongs at the end of each side of the basket. Now carefully move the rotisserie catch lever to the right to release.

Slowly pull the rotisserie basket toward you, then release the rotisserie catch lever.

Carefully slide the basket along the guides with the rotisserie fetch tool and remove from the cooking chamber.

While still wearing the oven mitts, set the rotisserie fetch tool aside and remove the lid of the basket. The fries should be golden brown and crispy. Transfer the French fries to a serving bowl and season with salt.

Note: For those who enjoy sweet potato fries, the AirFry function works just as well. Simply peel and slice a large sweet potato into French-fry sticks. Toss with a little vegetable oil and place them into the rotisserie basket. Follow the same instructions as above, but set for twenty to twenty-five minutes, depending on how many sweet potato fries you are air frying. After the allotted time, the sweet potato fries should be nice and crisp on the outside and moist and tender in the inside.

FUNCTION 2

ROASTING

The Roasting function of the Instant Vortex Plus Air Fryer Oven is another popular and often used function. Online reviewers seem to enjoy roasting chickens in this revolutionary appliance, something that is difficult to achieve in a roasting pan in a conventional oven. When you use the rotisserie spit, roasted chickens turn slowly, promoting thorough cooking inside and a rendered, juicy skin outside. Please keep in mind, however, that the Instant Vortex Plus Air Fryer Oven has a four-pound weight limit when you prepare whole chickens rotisserie style. Anything heavier, and you risk overloading the capacity of the motor, while smaller birds like a guinea hen or quail will have plenty of room.

Let's begin by walking through the general steps for how to use the Roasting function. We'll then look at several examples, including how to roast a whole chicken, prime rib, and potatoes.

To begin:

1. Select the Roast function from the Control Panel display.
2. Select the temperature. The temperature will default to 400°F. To increase or decrease the temperature, press the up (+) and down (-) arrows from the Temp function located on the left side of the oven.
3. Select the cooking time. To increase or decrease the cooking time, press the up (+) and down (-) arrows from the Time function located on the right side of the oven.
4. Press Start to begin. The digital display will illuminate the word ON.
5. Prepare your ingredients.

6. When the Instant Vortex Plus Air Fryer Oven reaches temperature, the digital display will alert you to "Add Food," accompanied by a series of beeps.

7. Add the food, making sure the drip pan is securely in place. The great advantage of the Instant Vortex Plus Air Fryer Oven, unlike other air fryers, is that the appliance comes with two cooking trays and a rotisserie, allowing you to cook a lot more food than with a standard air fryer.

8. Close the glass air fryer door to begin cooking.

9. Rather than your stopping or opening up a lid to check on your food, the Instant Vortex Plus Air Fryer Oven will automatically alert you to "Turn Food." At this time, turn the food and/or rotate the cooking trays, if using, for even cooking. Not all food needs turning or rotating, as when you're using the rotisserie, so this alert depends on what specifically you are roasting. If you do not turn the food, no problem. Cooking will proceed after 10 seconds, whether the food has been turned or not.

10. Close the glass air fryer door to resume cooking.

11. When there is only one minute of cooking time remaining, the cook time will count down in seconds. When no time is left, the word COOL will be displayed, accompanied by a series of beeps, followed by the fan being activated to cool the oven.

12. When the Instant Vortex Plus Air Fryer Oven is finished cooling, the word END will illuminate on the display, accompanied by another series of beeps.

13. Wearing your oven mitts, carefully open the glass air fryer door and remove the food and trays/rotisserie basket/other from the cooking chamber. Use caution, because the door and accessories will be hot.

Roasting Tip: Because there isn't much wiggle room for a four-pound chicken, make sure to trim and truss your bird before you rotisserie. This will save space while avoiding the wings and legs from flopping around during the cooking process.

Roasting Examples:

Roasting a Whole Chicken with the Rotisserie Spit

Believe it or not, many people who have purchased the Instant Vortex Plus Air Fryer Oven do so for its ability to roast a whole chicken. No need to buy a rotisserie chicken from your grocery store anymore. Now you can rotisserie yourself.

When roasting a whole chicken, begin by selecting a chicken that weighs no more than four pounds, as this is the maximum weight the Instant Vortex Plus Air Fryer Oven can hold. That said, you may find a whole chicken at your local grocery store that is just under five pounds. Often, if you remove the packaging, giblets, and some extra fat, you'll get the chicken to four pounds or less. Also, keep in mind that a four-pound bird may be small enough for the Instant Vortex Plus Air Fryer Oven, but probably not large enough to leave any leftovers for a family of four.

Next, use some butcher's twine or kitchen string to secure the chicken wings and legs to its body. If you don't, the wings and legs will flop repeatedly as the chicken rotates during the rotisserie setting, eventually tearing away.

Once the bird's appendages are securely in place, insert the rotisserie spit arm included with the Instant Vortex Plus Air Fryer Oven. Next, unscrew the two set screws located on each rotisserie fork (this can easily be done by hand) and slide the forks (screw side on top) onto both ends of the rotisserie spit, ensuring the fork prongs are inserted into the bird to secure it in place. Then tighten each fork screw to secure the forks to the rotisserie spit.

With the bird secure, spray the chicken on all sides with some avocado or cooking oil. Then season liberally with salt and pepper, or your favorite seasoning (Lawry's Seasoned Salt, lemon pepper, etc.).

Insert the drip pan, if you haven't already done so, and make sure it is securely in place.

Holding the rotisserie catch lever to the right, slide the rotisserie spit with the chicken along the guides in the cooking chamber. Use the rotisserie fetch that's included with the Instant Vortex Plus Air Fryer Oven to insert and remove the rotisserie spit.

Align the rotisserie spit of either accessory with the hole in the center of the rotisserie catch, then release the rotisserie catch lever to lock the spit arm firmly in place. You may have to wiggle the arm a little so the left arm "locks" inside the rotisserie catch. You will hear a locking noise, confirming the rotisserie spit is locked in place. Wiggle the rotisserie spit to make sure it's held firmly in place on both sides of the cooking chamber. Also, make sure the chicken is centered in the cooking chamber. If not, slide the chicken to the left or right until it is perfectly centered.

Once the chicken is centered and securely in place, close the glass air fryer door.

Select Roast from the Control Panel display.

Next, select the desired cooking temperature by touching the temperature +/- control on the left side. For roasting a four-pound chicken, select 380°F.

Select the desired cooking time by touching the time +/- control on the right side. For roasting a four-pound chicken, select forty-five minutes.

Next, touch the Rotate button to turn the rotisserie rotation on for a nice, even roast.

Then press Start.

When finished cooking, and wearing your oven mitts, carefully open the glass air fryer door. Use caution, because the door and accessories will be hot.

To release the rotisserie spit from either the rotisserie spit and forks or the rotisserie basket, insert the rotisserie fetch tool to "hook" the spit arms on each side. Now carefully move the rotisserie catch lever to the right to release.

Slowly pull the rotisserie spit and forks or the rotisserie basket toward you, then release the rotisserie catch lever.

Carefully slide the spit arms back along the guides to remove the rotisserie accessory and food from the cooking chamber.

Using an instant read thermometer, check the internal temperature of the chicken (best to insert the thermometer probe into the thickest part of the thigh of the chicken for the most accurate read). The internal temperature should read 170°F.

Let the chicken rest for about ten minutes. Remove the butcher's twine before serving.

Roasting a Prime Rib with the Rotisserie Spit

If you are successful preparing a rotisserie-style chicken, now let's try it with a quality cut of beef.

For this example, select a high-quality roast of prime rib from your butcher. Make sure the roast, like the chicken example, is not more than four pounds, as the maximum weight the Instant Vortex Plus Air Fryer Oven can support is four pounds of meat.

Season the roast liberally on all sides with salt and pepper or your favorite steak seasoning. This will form the meat's savory crust.

Using a long wooden or metal kebab skewer with a sharpened point, push the skewer all the way through the middle of the roast until the point comes out on the other side. Remove the skewer and replace with the rotisserie spit arm included with the Instant Vortex Plus Air Fryer Oven. (Note: because the spit arm does not have a sharp point, it's helpful to guide the spit arm by first inserting a sharp rod into the meat before inserting the spit arm.)

Next, unscrew the two set screws located on each rotisserie fork. This can easily be done by hand. Now slide the forks (screw side on top) onto both ends of the rotisserie spit, ensuring the fork prongs are inserted into the roast to secure it in place. Then tighten each fork screw to secure the forks to the rotisserie spit.

Insert the drip pan, if you haven't already done so, and make sure it is securely in place.

Holding the rotisserie catch lever to the right, slide the rotisserie spit with the roast along the guides in the cooking chamber. Use the rotisserie fetch that's included with the Instant Vortex Plus Air Fryer Oven to insert and remove the rotisserie spit after cooking.

Align the left side of the rotisserie spit with the hole in the center of the rotisserie catch, then release the rotisserie catch lever to lock the spit arm firmly in place. You may have to wiggle the arm a little so the accessory "locks" inside the rotisserie catch. You will hear a locking noise, confirming the rotisserie spit is locked in place. Wiggle the roast to make sure it's held firmly in place on both sides of the cooking chamber.

Once the roast is secured in place, close the glass air fryer door.

Select Roast from the Control Panel display.

Next, select the desired cooking temperature by touching the temperature +/- control on the left side. For this four-pound prime rib, let's begin with 375°F for twenty minutes, and then 300°F for ten minutes. (Note: The maximum temperature you can cook with the Instant Vortex Plus Air Fryer Oven is 400°F).

Select the desired cooking time by touching the time +/- control on the right side. Again, we're starting with twenty minutes, then ten minutes at the reduced temperature. (Note: The maximum time you can cook with the Instant Vortex Plus Air Fryer Oven is one hour. For longer cooking times, you will have to wait until the one hour is up before adding additional time.)

Next, touch the Rotate button to turn on the rotisserie rotation for a nice, even roast.

Then press Start.

After twenty minutes, reduce the temperature to 300°F and set the time for ten minutes. Check the meat's internal thermometer using a kitchen thermometer. We're looking for an internal temperature of 115°F for medium-rare. Continue to roast in ten-minute increments until the desired internal temperature is reached.

When cooking is finished, and wearing your oven mitts, carefully open the glass air fryer door. Use caution, because the door and accessories will be hot.

To release the rotisserie spit, insert the rotisserie fetch tool to "hook" the spit arms on each side of the roast. Now carefully move the rotisserie catch lever to the right to release.

Slowly pull the rotisserie spit and roast toward you, then release the rotisserie catch lever.

Carefully slide the spit arms back along the guides to remove the roast from the cooking chamber.

Place the roast on a pan or serving platter and cover with aluminum foil for about fifteen minutes. After the resting period, remove the rotisserie forks and spit and carve the roast.

Roasting Potatoes Using the Rotisserie Basket

Since you're learning how to use the Roast function for cooking a chicken or a roast of beef, it's best we also include how to roast an accompanying side dish. For this example, let's roast some potatoes while illustrating the Roasting function and the rotisserie basket.

Let's begin by making some Thyme-Roasted Potatoes. First, slice one pound of small red potatoes in half. This will make about three or four servings. Place the sliced potatoes in a bowl and toss with 1 tablespoon of olive oil, 1½ teaspoons fresh thyme, ½ teaspoon salt, and ⅛ teaspoon black pepper.

Next, transfer the seasoned potatoes inside the rotisserie basket. Because the basket doesn't stand upright on the counter (due to the prongs mounted at the ends of the basket), find a suitable bowl and set the basket inside the bowl for upright support and balance.

Like we did when air frying French fries, make sure not to overcrowd or overfill the basket or the potatoes will steam instead of air frying. The basket should comfortably hold all the potatoes for this recipe (about 1½ pounds of small red potatoes). A good rule of thumb is to only fill your basket half full with food.

Secure the rotisserie basket lid on top by aligning the tab on the rotisserie basket with the notch in the lid. Turn the lid clockwise to "lock" it in place. A "lock-unlock" diagram on top of the lid will help you turn the lid in the proper direction.

Make sure the drip pan is in place on the bottom of the cooking chamber before air frying.

To begin, press the Roast button from the Control Panel display, set the temperature to 400°F, and time for twenty minutes.

When the Instant Vortex Plus Air Fryer Oven reaches temperature, the digital display will alert you to "Add Food," accompanied by a series of beeps.

Open the glass air frying door. Note: To prevent the oil from the potatoes dripping onto the glass door, place a silicone mat (see accessories, page 12) over the door.

Holding the rotisserie catch lever to the right, slide the rotisserie basket along the guides in the cooking chamber. Use the rotisserie fetch that's included with the Instant Vortex Plus Air Fryer Oven to insert and remove the rotisserie basket after cooking.

Align the ends of the rotisserie basket with the hole in the center of the rotisserie catch, then release the rotisserie catch lever to lock the basket firmly in place. You may have to wiggle the basket a little so the accessory "locks" inside the rotisserie catch. You will hear a locking noise, confirming the rotisserie basket is locked in place. Wiggle the rotisserie basket to make sure it's held firmly in place on both sides of the cooking chamber.

Once the basket is secured in place, remove the silicone mat (if using) and close the glass air fryer door.

Press the Rotate button so the basket will rotate while the potatoes roast.

Press the Start button. The Instant Vortex Plus Air Fryer Oven will then display the word ON as the basket begins to rotate for twenty minutes.

When the cooking is complete, the Instant Vortex Plus Air Fryer Oven will automatically switch to "Cool" mode and then display the word END.

Wearing your oven mitts, carefully open the glass air fryer door. Use caution, because the door and accessories will be hot.

To release the rotisserie basket, insert the rotisserie fetch tool to "hook" the prongs at the end of each side of the basket. Now carefully move the rotisserie catch lever to the right to release.

Slowly pull the rotisserie basket toward you, then release the rotisserie catch lever.

Carefully slide the basket along the guides with the rotisserie fetch tool and remove from the cooking chamber.

While still wearing the oven mitts, set the rotisserie fetch tool aside and remove the lid of the basket. Transfer the roasted potatoes to a serving bowl. Sprinkle with 1 tablespoon fresh lemon zest and toss well before serving.

FUNCTION 3

BROILING

The Broiling function with the Instant Vortex Plus Air Fryer Oven seems simple enough. The temperature is already set to the maximum, at 400°F, so all you have to do is set the time and add the food when instructed. This method for broiling is a lot quicker than broiling under the heat source of your kitchen oven, although 400°F is the maximum heat in the Instant Vortex Plus Air Fryer Oven along with relatively limited space.

When broiling foods in the Instant Vortex Plus Air Fryer Oven, you may have to go through some trial and error to achieve perfect results.

Obviously, no one wants to waste time or food, so let's try the Broiling function with some salmon, steak, and asparagus. We'll even toast some bread and see what happens. Let's begin with the following set of overall instructions:

1. Select the Broiling function from the Control Panel display.

2. The temperature for broiling is already set to 400°F, the maximum temperature setting with the Instant Vortex Plus Air Fryer Oven. Note: The oven will not allow you to adjust temperature. This may seem confusing, since the Cooking Table in the back of the Getting Started Guide that comes with your oven says to broil/bake asparagus, for example, at 370°F. Disregard this.

3. Select the cooking time. To increase or decrease the cooking time, press the up (+) and down (-) arrows from the Time function located on the right side of the oven.

4. Press Start to begin. The digital display will illuminate the word ON.

5. Prepare your ingredients.

6. When the Instant Vortex Plus Air Fryer Oven reaches temperature, the digital display will alert you to "Add Food," accompanied by a series of beeps.

7. Add the food, making sure the drip pan is securely in place.

8. Close the glass air fryer door to begin cooking.

9. Rather than your stopping or opening up a lid to check on your food, the Instant Vortex Plus Air Fryer Oven will automatically alert you to "Turn Food." At this time, turn the food and/or rotate the Cooking Trays, if using, for even cooking. Not all food needs turning or rotating, so this alert depends on what specifically you are broiling. If you do not turn the food, no problem. Cooking will proceed after ten seconds, whether the food has been turned or not.

10. Close the glass air fryer door to resume cooking.

11. When there is only one minute of cooking time remaining, the cook time will count

down in seconds. When no time is left, the word COOL will be displayed, accompanied by a series of beeps, followed by the fan being activated to cool the oven.

12. When the Instant Vortex Plus Air Fryer Oven is finished cooling, the word END will illuminate on the display, accompanied by another series of beeps.

13. Wearing your oven mitts, carefully open the glass air fryer door and remove the food and cooking tray from the cooking chamber. Use caution, because the door and accessories will be hot.

Broiling Tip: One important thing to keep in mind when broiling with the Instant Vortex Plus Air Fryer Oven is that you don't receive a reminder to "Turn Food." Even though you don't have to turn most foods when you broil, if you do (or want to) turn your food, you will need to set your own timer. A simple kitchen- or egg timer will do just fine.

Broiling Examples:

Broiling Salmon

Broiling is one of the easiest, most popular ways to cook fish, and almost any type of fish can be broiled. The key is to not overcook, or in this case overbroil, your fish.

All fish headed under the broiler should be seasoned at least twenty minutes prior to broiling, forty minutes if the fish fillets are quite thick.

For this example, let's use two fillets of Alaska wild salmon, at five ounces each. Rub each fillet with a little olive oil and sprinkle with salt and pepper, or whatever seasoning you prefer, and place in the refrigerator for twenty minutes.

Make sure the drip pan is securely in place. Press the Broil function from the Control Panel display when you're ready to begin cooking. Remember, the temperature is already programmed to 400°F. Set the time for five minutes, then press the Start button. The Instant Vortex Plus Air Fryer Oven will then display the word ON. Do not add the fish just yet. Allow the oven to preheat.

While the Instant Vortex Plus Air Fryer Oven is preheating, now is a good time to arrange the two salmon fillets on the cooking tray, skin side down.

When the Instant Vortex Plus Air Fryer Oven reaches temperature, the digital display will alert you to "Add Food," accompanied by a series of beeps. Open the glass air fryer door (you don't have to press or cancel anything), slide the cooking tray with the salmon fillets to the top rack, and close the door. The Instant Vortex Plus Air Fryer Oven will automatically start and count down for five minutes. If needed, press the Light function to illuminate the inside of the cooking chamber.

When the broiling time is finished, the Instant Vortex Plus Air Fryer Oven will automatically switch to "Cool" mode and then display the word END.

Wearing your oven mitts, open the glass air fryer door and remove the cooking tray with the broiled salmon and let the fish rest for several minutes before serving. Use caution, because the door and accessories will be hot. Note: The fish will continue to cook once it is removed from the oven. This fish should be cooked to a perfect medium to medium-rare.

Again, a good kitchen practice after cooking is to keep the glass air fryer door open. This allows the oven to cool much quicker before cleaning.

Broiling Steak

Like broiling fish, perfecting a steak using the Broiling function with the Instant Vortex Plus Air Fryer Oven may take a little trial and error, since there are many different kinds of beef cuts. Remember, you can also always put the steak back in and broil it longer if it's under-cooked, but there's nothing you can do once it's overcooked. When in doubt, broil for less time and check the steak using a cooking or grilling thermometer or the somewhat reliable "touch" test (you can find these easy no-thermometer touch-tests online).

For this example, let's broil one eight-ounce prime filet mignon to medium-rare. If you prefer a medium center, you can broil a little longer. Rub the filet of beef with a little olive oil and sprinkle with Lawry's Seasoned Salt, or whatever steak seasoning you prefer. Brush the top of the filet with a little melted butter and let the steak rest for about one hour or until the steak comes to room temperature.

Make sure the drip pan is securely in place. Press the Broil function from the Control Panel display. Remember the temperature is already set to 400°F. Set the time for eight minutes (ten minutes for medium), then press the Start button. The Instant Vortex Plus Air Fryer Oven will then display the word ON. Do not add the meat just yet. Allow the oven to preheat.

While the Instant Vortex Plus Air Fryer Oven is preheating, now is a good time to arrange the steak on the cooking tray and pour yourself a glass of wine.

When the Instant Vortex Plus Air Fryer Oven reaches temperature, the digital display will alert you to "Add Food," accompanied by a series of beeps. Open the glass air fryer door (you don't have to press or cancel anything), slide the cooking tray with the steak to the top rack, and close the door. The Instant Vortex Plus Air Fryer Oven will automatically start and count down for eight minutes. If needed, press the Light function to illuminate the inside of the cooking chamber.

During the broiling process, the Instant Vortex Plus Air Fryer Oven may automatically alert you to "Turn Food." You don't need to. Simply ignore this message, and the broiling time will continue counting down.

When the broiling time is finished, the Instant Vortex Plus Air Fryer Oven will automatically switch to "Cool" mode and then display the word END.

Wearing your oven mitts, open the glass air fryer door and remove the cooking tray with the broiled steak. Use caution, because the door and accessories will be hot. Let the meat rest for several minutes before serving. The steak should have a nice char on the outside, and the meat should be tender, juicy, and flavorful when cut into.

Again, a good kitchen practice after cooking is to keep the glass air fryer door open. This allows the oven to cool much quicker before cleaning.

Broiling Asparagus

It's nice to enjoy perfectly broiled fish or steak with a vegetable, so let's broil some asparagus to accompany your meal. Again, there will likely be some trial and error when it comes to perfecting the broiling time because there are so many different kinds of vegetables out there.

Make sure the drip pan is securely in place. Press the Broil function from the Control Panel display. Remember the temperature is already set to 400°F. Set the time to eight minutes, then press the Start button. The Instant Vortex Plus Air Fryer Oven will then display the word ON. Do not add the asparagus yet. Allow the oven to preheat, which will take about two or three minutes.

While the Instant Vortex Plus Air Fryer Oven is preheating, now is a good time to prep the asparagus.

Wash and dry sixteen to eighteen spears of fresh asparagus and trim off and discard the rough ends. Add the asparagus to a large bowl and toss with a little olive oil, Parmesan cheese, salt, and a squeeze of lemon juice. Toss well and transfer the asparagus to one of the cooking trays, making sure none of the asparagus spears overlap one another.

When the Instant Vortex Plus Air Fryer Oven reaches temperature, the digital display will alert you to "Add Food," accompanied by a series of beeps. Open the glass air fryer door (you don't have to press or cancel anything), slide the cooking tray with the asparagus to the middle rack, and close the door. Instant Vortex Plus Air Fryer Oven will automatically start and count down for eight minutes. If needed, press the Light function to illuminate the inside of the cooking chamber.

During the broiling process, the Instant Vortex Plus Air Fryer Oven will automatically alert you to "Turn Food." At this time, don your oven mitts and open the glass air fryer door and remove the cooking tray with the asparagus. Note: Keep the oven door open. If you don't, the broiling time will continue counting down. With a spatula or pair of tongs, shuffle the asparagus a little so they are able to broil and char evenly. Then return the cooking tray with asparagus back to the middle rack and close the glass air fryer door to resume broiling.

When the broiling time is finished, the Instant Vortex Plus Air Fryer Oven will automatically switch to "Cool" mode and then display the word END.

Wearing your oven mitts, open the glass air fryer door and remove the cooking tray with the broiled asparagus. Use caution, because the door and accessories will be hot. The asparagus should be nicely charred and the stalks not limp or mushy.

Again, a good kitchen practice after cooking is to keep the glass air fryer door open. This allows the oven to cool much quicker before cleaning.

Toasting Bread

Most of us like toast, especially garlic bread/toast with dinner. With kitchen counter space often being limited to what we put on it, the Instant Vortex Plus Air Fryer Oven serves as a great replacement for the toaster or toaster oven.

You may have noticed that on the original Instant Vortex Plus Air Fryer Oven box, the manufacturer says you can toast with this appliance. However, there isn't any mention of toasting in the Instant Vortex Plus Air Fryer Oven Safety, Maintenance & Warranty booklet or the Getting Started Guide. No need to worry, toasting is simple with the broiling feature.

Make sure the drip pan is securely in place. Press the Broil function from the Control Panel display. Remember, the temperature is already set to 400°F. Set the time for two minutes for a light toast (three minutes for a dark toast), then press the Start button. The Instant Vortex Plus Air Fryer Oven will then display the word ON. Do not add any bread yet. Allow the oven to preheat, which will take about two or three minutes.

While the Instant Vortex Plus Air Fryer Oven is preheating, now is a good time to prep your food being toasted, such as slicing some fresh baked bread and brushing with melted butter, garlic, and a sprinkle of fresh Italian parsley. You can also add some fresh grated Parmesan cheese and a sprinkle of paprika. Place the bread slices on one of the cooking trays.

When the Instant Vortex Plus Air Fryer Oven says to "Add Food," and the timer goes off, open the glass air fryer door (you don't have to press or cancel anything), slide the cooking tray with the bread slices to the middle rack, and close the door. The Instant Vortex Plus Air Fryer Oven will automatically start and count down for two minutes. If needed, press the Light function to illuminate the inside of the cooking chamber.

When the broiling time is finished, the Instant Vortex Plus Air Fryer Oven will automatically switch to "Cool" mode and then display the word END.

Wearing your oven mitts, open the glass air fryer door and remove the cooking tray with the toasted garlic bread. Use caution, because the door and accessories will be hot. The Instant Vortex Plus Air Fryer Oven will toast both sides of the bread, so there's no need to turn or flip during the broiling process.

Again, a good kitchen practice after cooking is to keep the glass air fryer door open. This allows the oven to cool much quicker before cleaning.

FUNCTION 4

BAKING

Baking in the Instant Vortex Plus Air Fryer Oven is much easier and quicker than in the conventional oven, which is a plus for home cooks. However, not every pan fits inside the countertop appliance. Please review the additional accessories (page 10) for what will work when baking. For example, the Instant Vortex Plus Air Fryer Oven comfortably holds an 8x8-inch baking dish, an eight-inch round cake or pie pan, or a 1.5-quart ceramic baking dish, whether it is oval, round, or square. Cooking times can be slightly different as well, so, again, trial and error will lead to perfection rather than relying on the package directions when it comes to temperature and time. Some home cooks believe the Instant Vortex Plus Air Fryer Oven runs hotter than their kitchen oven when it comes to baking, so watch your baking time. Parchment paper holds up to baking in the Instant Vortex Plus Air Fryer Oven, which means you can line the cooking trays when baking such items as cookies. Speaking of cookies, a handful of home bakers baked some cookies using the Instant Vortex Plus Air Fryer Oven. Their first batch followed the time and temperature recommended on the package. They came out overdone. A second batch was baked twenty-five degrees cooler and yielded much better results. Another case of trial and error required to get things right when converting from the manufacturer's directions.

In this chapter, we will go over the general baking instructions before baking several items, including a cake, some muffins, and the classic baked potato.

To begin:

1. Select the Baking function from the Control Panel display.

2. Select the cooking temperature. To increase or decrease the cooking temperature, press the up (+) and down (-) arrows from the Temp function located on the left side of the oven.

3. Select the cooking time. To increase or decrease the cooking time, press the up (+) and down (-) arrows from the Time function located on the right side of the oven.

4. Press Start to begin. The digital display will illuminate the word ON.

5. Prepare your ingredients.

6. When the Instant Vortex Plus Air Fryer Oven reaches temperature, the digital display will alert you to "Add Food," accompanied by a series of beeps.

7. Add the food, making sure the drip pan is securely in place.

8. Close the glass air fryer door to begin cooking.

9. Rather than your stopping or opening up a lid to check on your food, the Instant Vortex Plus Air Fryer Oven will automatically alert you to "Turn Food." At

this time, turn the food and/or rotate the cooking trays, if using, for even cooking. Not all food needs turning or rotating, so this alert depends on what specifically you are baking. If you do not turn the food, no problem. Cooking will proceed after ten seconds, whether the food has been turned or not.

10. Close the glass air fryer door to resume baking.

11. When there is only one minute of baking time remaining, the cook time will count down in seconds. When no time is left, the word COOL will be displayed, accompanied by a series of beeps, followed by the fan being activated to cool the oven.

12. When the Instant Vortex Plus Air Fryer Oven is finished cooling, the word END will illuminate on the display, along with another series of beeps.

13. Wearing your oven mitts, carefully open the glass air fryer door and remove the baked item from the cooking chamber.

Use caution, because the door and accessories will be hot.

Baking Tips: One trick to keep in mind when baking is that if your cake pan or bowl is a tad larger than the cooking tray, simply remove the tray and flip it upside down. The underside of the tray does not have a "lip," so flipping over the tray will give you a bit more room should your bakeware be a little larger than the tray itself.

Baking Examples:
Baking a Cake

No matter what the occasion, there's nothing like baking a cake for family, friends, or just yourself. Now you can bake a cake even more easily with the Instant Vortex Plus Air Fryer Oven, and in about half the time of a standard convection oven.

For this quick and easy demonstration, let's indulge our senses by starting with an all-around favorite: 1 box of Betty Crocker Super Moist Favorites Butter Recipe Yellow Cake Mix. If you're an avid baker, feel free to make from scratch, but you can't go wrong when using a Betty Crocker mix.

Begin by pouring the cake mix into a large mixing bowl. Next, add to the bowl a package of the regular 3.4-ounce Jell-O instant vanilla pudding, then add 4 whole eggs, ½ cup vegetable oil, and ½ cup cold water.

Using a stand mixer, electric hand mixer, or an old-fashioned whisk, whisk until the mixture comes together and forms a smooth batter, but do not overmix. Now, with a rubber spatula, give the batter a good stir. This ensures all the dry ingredients are incorporated.

Grease a high-sided eight-inch cake pan with butter or nonstick cooking spray. You can also use a small Bundt pan if it fits inside the Instant Vortex Plus Air Fryer Oven. Next, line the bottom of the pan with a round piece of parchment paper. Note: To help reduce the heat of the pan and eliminate your cakes from overbrowning in the Instant Vortex Plus Air Fryer Oven, make a "foil collar." Do so by taking a strip of aluminum foil and folding it in half a couple times to thicken the foil, then wrap the collar around the edge of your baking pan. To secure, fold the foil ends together and tighten against the pan.

Using a measuring cup, scoop two heaping cups of batter into the pan. Note: The batter makes four cups, but because of the eight-inch pan for baking inside the Instant Vortex Plus Air Fryer Oven, only two cups will suffice, allowing you to make two cakes.

Using the kitchen spatula, smooth out the batter in the pan and set aside.

Open the glass air fryer door and remove the cooking trays and drip pan. Now, take one of the cooking trays, flip it over so the "lip" is not exposed, and place it on the bottom of the cooking chamber where the drip pan usually sits. Close the door.

Select the Baking function from the Control Panel display.

Set the cooking temperature to 325°F and the cooking time to twenty-five minutes. Then press Start.

When the Instant Vortex Plus Air Fryer Oven reaches temperature, the digital display will alert you to "Add Food," accompanied by a series of beeps.

Open the glass air fryer door and insert the cake pan.

Close the glass air fryer door to begin baking.

During the baking cycle, the Instant Vortex Plus Air Fryer Oven will automatically alert you to "Turn Food." For baking this cake, there's no need to turn anything. Simply ignore the alert. The baking will resume after ten seconds.

When there is only one minute of baking time remaining, the cook time will count down in seconds. When no time is left, the word COOL will be displayed, accompanied by a series of beeps, followed by the fan being activated to cool the oven.

When the Instant Vortex Plus Air Fryer Oven is finished cooling, the word END will illuminate on the display, along with another series of beeps.

Wearing your oven mitts, carefully open the glass air fryer door and remove the cake pan from the cooking chamber. Use caution, because the door and accessories will be hot.

Using the "toothpick" method, or a long wooden skewer for easier testing, insert into the center of the cake and remove. The toothpick should come out clean. If not, continue to bake until the center is cooked through.

While the cake is cooling, make whatever frosting or glaze you like, spread on top of the cake, slice, and enjoy with some whipped cream or ice cream.

Baking Muffins

For another quick and easy demonstration, let's stick to what works, this time 1 box of Betty Crocker Muffin Mix. Of course, if you're an avid baker, feel free to ignore the batter preparation steps and make yours from scratch.

Begin by pouring the muffin mix into a large mixing bowl. Use a rubber kitchen spatula to break up any dry clumps. Next, follow the directions on the package. For this example, we're using a pouch of the Betty Crocker Triple Berry Muffin Mix. This means we add ½ cup milk. Stir until the batter is smooth.

Next, grease a muffin pan that fits inside the Instant Vortex Plus Air Fryer Oven with non-stick cooking spray. Note: If you like the crispy taste of the muffin, do not use muffin liners. You can use a mini-muffin pan, a standard four-count muffin pan, a deep silicone muffin tray, or individual silicone baking cups (see accessories page 11). Any muffin pan, tray, or cup will work so long as it fits comfortably inside the oven. Now, add the muffin batter. For this example, we're using the mini-muffin pan that holds a dozen mini-muffins. This means two teaspoons of batter in each pregreased cup.

Open the glass air fryer door and insert one of the Cooking Trays on the lower rack, then close the door.

Select the Baking function from the Control Panel display.

Set the cooking temperature to 360°F and the cooking time to six minutes. Then press Start.

When the Instant Vortex Plus Air Fryer Oven reaches temperature, the digital display will alert you to "Add Food," accompanied by a series of beeps.

Open the glass air fryer door and insert the muffin pan on top of the Cooking Tray.

Close the glass air fryer door to begin baking.

During the baking cycle, the Instant Vortex Plus Air Fryer Oven will automatically alert you to "Turn Food." For baking the muffins, there's no need to turn anything. Simply ignore the alert. The baking will resume after ten seconds.

When there is only one minute of baking time remaining, the cook time will count down in seconds. When no time is left, the word COOL will be displayed, accompanied by a series of beeps, followed by the fan being activated to cool the oven.

When the Instant Vortex Plus Air Fryer Oven is finished cooling, the word END will illuminate on the display, along with another series of beeps.

Wearing your oven mitts, carefully open the glass air fryer door and remove the muffin pan from the cooking chamber. Use caution, because the door and accessories will be hot.

Using the "toothpick" method, or a long wooden skewer for easier testing, insert into the center of the cake and remove. The toothpick should come out clean. If not, continue to bake until the center is cooked through.

To cool, remove the muffins from the pan and turn them upside down for several minutes before arranging them on a serving platter to enjoy. The muffins should be golden brown on top with soft, moist bottoms.

Baking Potatoes

For serving up restaurant-quality baked potatoes, with that delicious crispy skin yet light and fluffy inside, look no further than the Instant Vortex Plus Air Fryer Oven. What's also enjoyable is the short cooking time. Like other foods cooked in the Instant Vortex Plus Air Fryer Oven, baking potatoes is much more efficient and faster than baking them in a standard convection oven.

To begin, select two to four large russet potatoes, depending on how many you are baking. Russets are a great go-to potato for baking because they are large and have the perfect starch consistency that bakes up nicely. After cleaning the potatoes and patting them dry, rub a little olive (or vegetable) oil on each potato, coating all of the skins. This will help the potatoes from drying out while crisping the skin simultaneously.

Place the potatoes on the cooking trays. If you're baking three or four potatoes, use both trays. You don't want to crowd the trays, and there should be plenty of space between the potatoes. This will allow the oven's hot air to circulate and bake the potatoes evenly.

Once potatoes are slathered in oil, prick them with a fork and sprinkle each one with a little salt, garlic powder, seasoning salt, or whatever you like.

Make sure the drip pan is in the bottom of the oven.

Select the Baking function from the Control Panel display.

Set the cooking temperature to 400°F and then set the cooking time. The time will depend on how many potatoes you are baking and the size of the potatoes. For this exercise, we are baking two ten-ounce russet potatoes for forty-five minutes.

Then press Start.

When the Instant Vortex Plus Air Fryer Oven reaches temperature, the digital display will alert you to "Add Food," accompanied by a series of beeps.

Open the glass air fryer door and insert the cooking tray in the middle rack with the seasoned potatoes, making sure there is plenty of space between the two potatoes.

Close the glass air fryer door to begin baking.

When there is only one minute of baking time remaining, the cook time will count down in seconds. When no time is left, the word COOL will be displayed, accompanied by a series of beeps, followed by the fan being activated to cool the oven.

When the Instant Vortex Plus Air Fryer Oven is finished cooling, the word END will illuminate on the display, along with another series of beeps.

Wearing your oven mitts, carefully open the glass air fryer door and remove the cooking tray and potatoes from the cooking chamber. Use caution, because the door and accessories will be hot.

To test doneness, use a fork or knife inserted into the center of the potato. The potato is baked perfectly if the utensil slides easily in and out. If you find it a little hard for the utensil to penetrate the center of the potato, it needs more cooking time.

When finished baking, load the potato with your favorite toppings and enjoy.

FUNCTION 5

REHEATING

The reheat function of the Instant Vortex Plus Air Fryer Oven serves as a basic replacement for your microwave and is much quicker and efficient than reheating your leftovers on a kitchen burner or in the oven or under the broiler. With lower temperatures and no preheat times, the Instant Vortex Plus Air Fryer Oven is perfect to reheat your food without overcooking. Reheating in the air fryer also produces far better results. Your leftovers reheat to a perfect temperature while not compromising the texture of your food, as opposed to a microwave that often makes leftovers like pizza, bread, and sandwiches soft, limp, and chewy after a reheat. Without question, reheating leftovers with ease is a wonderful feature, especially for busy moms and dads on the go.

Let's look at the basic instructions for how to properly reheat your food, followed by a few reheating examples, including cold pizza, chili, and a chicken potpie.

To begin:

1. Select the Reheat function from the Control Panel display.
2. Select the cooking temperature. The default is 280°F. To increase or decrease the cooking temperature, press the up (+) and down (-) arrows from the Temp function located on the left side of the oven.
3. Select the cooking time. To increase or decrease the cooking time, press the up (+) and down (-) arrows from the Time function located on the right side of the oven.
4. Press Start to begin. The digital display will illuminate the word ON.

5. The oven will prompt you to "Add Food" right away.

6. Make sure the drip pan is securely in place and add the food.

7. Close the glass air fryer door to begin reheating.

8. When there is only one minute of cooking time remaining, the cook time will count down in seconds. When no time is left, the word COOL will be displayed, accompanied by a series of beeps, followed by the fan being activated to cool the oven.

9. When the Instant Vortex Plus Air Fryer Oven is finished cooling, the word END will illuminate on the display, along with another series of beeps.

10. Wearing your oven mitts, carefully open the glass air fryer door and remove the reheated food from the cooking chamber. Use caution, because the door and accessories will be hot.

Reheating Tip: Some cold leftovers just aren't meant to reheat in the Instant Vortex Plus Air Fryer Oven due to the long reheat times. For example, if you're thinking about reheating a bowl of your baked macaroni and cheese from the cold casserole dish in the refrigerator, it may take you thirty minutes. It may be quicker to reheat such items over the stove in less time. But if you're after convenience and not worried about time, then reheat away in the air fryer.

Reheating Examples

Reheating Pizza

For this example, let's reheat two slices of cold pizza pulled from the refrigerator.

Select the Reheat function from the Control Panel display.

Select the cooking temperature. The default is 280°F. To increase or decrease the cooking temperature, press the up (+) and down (-) arrows from the Temp function located on the left side of the oven. For reheating the two pieces of pizza, let's keep to the 280°F.

Select the cooking time. To increase or decrease the cooking time, press the up (+) and down (-) arrows from the Time function located on the right side of the oven. For reheating the two pieces of pizza, let's select three minutes.

Press Start to begin. The digital display will illuminate the word ON.

The oven will prompt you to "Add Food" right away.

Make sure the drip pan is securely in place and arrange the cold pizza on one of cooking trays. Place on the middle rack.

Close the glass air fryer door to begin reheating.

When there is only one minute of cooking time remaining, the cook time will count down in seconds. When no time is left, the word COOL will be displayed, accompanied by a series of beeps, followed by the fan being activated to cool the oven.

When the Instant Vortex Plus Air Fryer Oven is finished cooling, the word END will illuminate on the display, accompanied by another series of beeps.

Wearing your oven mitts, carefully open the glass air fryer door and remove the reheated pizza from the cooking chamber. Use caution, because the door and accessories will be hot.

The pizza slices should be crisp and hot.

Reheating Chili

Let's now try reheating a large bowl of cold chili from the refrigerator.

Select the Reheat function from the Control Panel display.

Select the cooking temperature. The default is 280°F. To increase or decrease the cooking temperature, press the up (+) and down (-) arrows from the Temp function located on the left side of the oven. For reheating the bowl of chili, let's increase the temperature to 290°F.

Select the cooking time. To increase or decrease the cooking time, press the up (+) and down (-) arrows from the Time function located on the right side of the oven. For reheating the bowl of chili, let's set the time to fifteen minutes.

Press Start to begin. The digital display will illuminate the word ON.

The oven will prompt you to "Add Food" right away.

Make sure the drip pan is securely in place and pour the chili in an oven-proof bowl. Place on one of the cooking trays and insert into the middle rack.

Close the glass air fryer door to begin reheating.

When there is only one minute of cooking time remaining, the cook time will count down in seconds. When no time is left, the word COOL will be displayed, accompanied by a series of beeps, followed by the fan being activated to cool the oven.

When the Instant Vortex Plus Air Fryer Oven is finished cooling, the word END will illuminate on the display, accompanied by another series of beeps.

Wearing your oven mitts, carefully open the glass air fryer door and remove the reheated bowl of chili from the cooking chamber. Use caution, because the door and accessories will be hot.

The bowl of chili should be nice and hot, and ready to eat.

Reheating a Chicken Potpie

For this last example, let's reheat an individual twelve-ounce potpie filled with tender chunks of chicken and vegetables in a roasted gravy. This potpie has been previously baked and placed in the refrigerator as a leftover and now needs to be reheated so it's hot and ready.

Select the Reheat function from the Control Panel display.

Select the cooking temperature. The default is 280°F. To increase or decrease the cooking temperature, press the up (+) and down (-) arrows from the Temp function located on the left side of the oven. For reheating this twelve-ounce potpie, let's increase the temperature to 350°F.

Select the cooking time. To increase or decrease the cooking time, press the up (+) and down (-) arrows from the Time function located on the right side of the oven. For reheating the potpie, let's select twenty minutes.

Press Start to begin. The digital display will illuminate the word ON.

The oven will prompt you to "Add Food" right away.

Make sure the drip pan is securely in place. Place the potpie on one of the cooking trays and insert into the middle rack.

Close the glass air fryer door to begin reheating.

When there is only one minute of cooking time remaining, the cook time will count down in seconds. When no time is left, the word COOL will be displayed, accompanied by a series of beeps, followed by the fan being activated to cool the oven.

When the Instant Vortex Plus Air Fryer Oven is finished cooling, the word END will illuminate on the display, accompanied by another series of beeps.

Wearing your oven mitts, carefully open the glass air fryer door and remove the reheated potpie from the cooking chamber. Use caution, because the door and accessories will be hot.

The potpie should be crisp and hot, with an internal temperature of 165° F, just like it was when previously baked.

FUNCTION 6

DEHYDRATING

Perhaps the most interesting feature of the Instant Vortex Plus Air Fryer Oven is the Dehydrate function, which you won't find with your typical toaster oven or other air fryer models. Making your own apple, banana, and fruit chips is a fun, convenient, do-it-yourself activity in the kitchen. Surprising your family and friends with homemade beef jerky and fruit roll-ups also makes the Instant Vortex Plus Air Fryer Oven a worthwhile investment. This is one of the redeeming qualities of the Instant Vortex Plus Air Fryer Oven. Dehydrating is simple to do, even for first-timers who haven't dehydrated before and are following a recipe along the way. For example, one home cook who hadn't dehydrated before followed a popular recipe online. She thinly sliced a two-pound top round and marinated the meat for about five hours before arranging the slices on the two cooking trays. She set the dehydrating temperature to 155°F and the time for three hours. Halfway through, she swapped the tray positions. After the time was up, she finished off the beef by baking the marinated slices at 275°F for ten minutes just to ensure food safety. She says the result was as good as she would buy in stores, and she did it all under four hours.

Let's look at the general instructions for how to dehydrate and then try a few examples, including how to dehydrate apple chips, beef jerky, and cauliflower at home.

To begin:

1. Select the Dehydrate function from the Control Panel display.
2. Select the cooking temperature. To increase or decrease the dehydrating temperature, press the up (+) and down

(-) arrows from the Temp function located on the left side of the oven.

3. Select the dehydrating time. To increase or decrease the cooking time, press the up (+) and down (-) arrows from the Time function located on the right side of the oven.

4. Press Start to begin. The digital display will illuminate the word ON.

5. Prepare your ingredients.

6. When the Instant Vortex Plus Air Fryer Oven reaches temperature, the digital display will alert you to "Add Food," accompanied by a series of beeps.

7. Add the food to be dehydrated, making sure the drip pan is securely in place.

8. Close the glass air fryer door to begin dehydrating.

9. When there is only one minute of dehydrating time remaining, the dehydrating time will count down in seconds. When no time is left, the word COOL will be displayed, accompanied by a series of audible beeps, followed by the fan being activated to cool the oven.

10. When the Instant Vortex Plus Air Fryer Oven is finished cooling, the word END will illuminate on the display, accompanied by another series of beeps.
11. Wearing your oven mitts, carefully open the glass air fryer door and remove the dehydrated food from the cooking chamber.

Dehydrating Tip: When making dehydrated foods like apple chips, do not slice the apples (or other fruit) too thin and do not use the top rack. When the moisture is removed from the apples, the dehydrated slices will lose their volume and weight. Placing them on the top rack is too close to the fan and will cause your dehydrated apple chips to fly around and burn inside the cooking chamber from the heating element. Try and keep the slices to just under ⅛ inch thick and use the middle and lower racks only, especially when dehydrating delicate foods.

Note that the Instant Vortex Plus Air Fryer Oven is rather loud. If you're planning to dehydrate for 6 or 10 hours, that's a lot of "whirring" of the motor, which can be somewhat of an annoyance if you're trying to nap, watch television, or read near the kitchen. Always remain nearby when Oven is in use.

Dehydrating Examples:

Apple Chips

Select the Dehydrate function from the Control Panel display.

Select the cooking temperature. For two trays of apple slices, select 135°F. To increase or decrease the dehydrating temperature, press the up (+) and down (-) arrows from the Temp function located on the left side of the oven.

Select the dehydrating time. For two trays of apple slices, select 6 to 8 hours, depending on how crisp you like your dehydrated apples. To increase or decrease the cooking time, press the up (+) and down (-) arrows from the Time function located on the right side of the oven.

Press Start to begin. The digital display will illuminate the word ON.

Next, prepare the apple chips by slicing one or two crisp, ripe apples into thin slices (about 1/8 inch thick). Arrange the slices on the cooking trays, making sure none of the apple slices are overlapping one another.

When the Instant Vortex Plus Air Fryer Oven reaches temperature, the digital display will alert you to "Add Food," accompanied by a series of beeps.

Add the cooking trays with the apple slices to the middle and bottom racks only, making sure the drip pan is securely in place. Note: Do not place the tray on the top rack.

Close the glass air fryer door to begin dehydrating.

After three hours of dehydrating time, wear your oven mitts and open the glass air fryer door. Change the Cooking Trays with the apple slices by moving the middle rack to the bottom rack and the bottom rack to the middle rack. Close the door to continue dehydrating.

When there is only one minute of dehydrating time remaining, the dehydrating time will count down in seconds. When no time is left, the word COOL will be displayed, accompanied by a series of beeps, followed by the fan being activated to cool the oven.

When the Instant Vortex Plus Air Fryer Oven is finished cooling, the word END will illuminate on the display, accompanied by another series of beeps.

Wearing your oven mitts, carefully open the glass air fryer door and remove the cooking trays and dehydrated apple slices from the cooking chamber. Let cool before serving.

Note: You can also dehydrate different fruits simultaneously. Try one cooking tray with slices of banana and one cooking tray with sliced apple. First, spray the trays with a nonstick cooking spray, as fruits like banana chips will stick during the dehydrating process. Place the tray with the bananas in the middle rack and the apple tray in the lower rack. Set temperature to 135°F for six to eight hours, depending on how crisp you like your dehydrated fruits. Halfway through, turn the banana chips over to the other side. You don't have to turn the apples.

Beef Jerky

Begin by prepping the beef. Using a sharp kitchen knife, thinly slice one pound of lean beef round into about twelve slices. Note: You can opt for thicker slices depending on how you like your beef jerky. Place the beef slices into a large bowl or ziplock bag and add ½ cup Worcestershire, ½ cup soy sauce, 2 teaspoons onion powder, 2 teaspoons honey, 1 teaspoon pepper, 1 teaspoon liquid smoke, and ½ teaspoon red pepper flakes. Mix well and allow the meat to marinate in the refrigerator for three to six hours.

Remove the beef slices from the marinade and arrange the slices on the two cooking trays, being careful not to overlap the slices. Open the glass air fryer oven and make sure the drip pan is in place. Place the cooking trays with the sliced beef on the top and bottom racks and close the glass air fryer door.

Select the Dehydrate function from the Control Panel display.

Select the cooking temperature. For two trays of beef slices, select 155°F. To increase or decrease the dehydrating temperature, press the up (+) and down (-) arrows from the Temp function located on the left side of the oven.

Select the dehydrating time. For two trays of beef slices, select three hours. To increase or decrease the cooking time, press the up (+) and down (-) arrows from the Time function located on the right side of the oven.

Press Start to begin. The digital display will illuminate the word ON.

After 1½ hours of dehydrating time, wear your oven mitts and open the glass air fryer door. Swap the cooking trays with the beef slices by moving the top rack to the bottom rack and the bottom rack to the top rack. Close the door to continue dehydrating.

When there is only one minute of dehydrating time remaining, the dehydrating time will count down in seconds. When no time is left, the word COOL will be displayed, accompanied by a series of beeps, followed by the fan being activated to cool the oven.

When the Instant Vortex Plus Air Fryer Oven is finished cooling, the word END will illuminate on the display, accompanied by another series of beeps.

Wearing your oven mitts, carefully open the glass air fryer door and remove the cooking trays and dehydrated beef slices from the cooking chamber. Let cool before serving. Note: For those who are extra cautious about food safety, you can further cook the beef jerky after it comes out from dehydrating. Simply set to Bake at 275°F and cook the jerky for ten minutes.

Cauliflower Popcorn

This is a unique item to dehydrate, so it had to be included here. This recipe comes from the manufacturer of the Instant Vortex Plus Air Fryer Oven and is definitely worth a try. After all, what could be more fun than taking a whole head of cauliflower and spicing it up with hot sauce, lime, and spices and then dehydrating it until it's crisp and crunchy?

Begin by prepping the cauliflower. Using a sharp kitchen knife, segment one head of cauliflower into very small crowns, about two pounds. Place the small crowns into a large bowl and add 2 tablespoons hot sauce, 1 tablespoon vegetable oil, 1 tablespoon lime juice, 1 tablespoon smoked paprika, 1 teaspoon cumin, and ½ teaspoon nutmeg. Mix well until the cauliflower crowns are well coated.

Arrange the cauliflower crowns on the two cooking trays in a single layer. Open the glass air fryer oven and make sure the drip pan is in place. Place the cooking trays with the cauli-flower crowns in the top and bottom racks and close the glass air fryer door.

Select the Dehydrate function from the Control Panel display.

Select the cooking temperature. For two trays of cauliflower crowns, select 130°F. To increase or decrease the dehydrating temperature, press the up (+) and down (-) arrows from the Temp function located on the left side of the oven.

Select the dehydrating time. For two trays of cauliflower crowns, select twelve hours. To increase or decrease the cooking time, press the up (+) and down (-) arrows from the Time func-tion located on the right side of the oven.

Press Start to begin. The digital display will illuminate the word ON.

After six hours of dehydrating time, wear your oven mitts and open the glass air fryer door. Change the cooking trays with the cau-liflower crowns by moving the top rack to the bottom rack and the bottom rack to the top rack. Close the door to continue dehydrating.

When there is only one minute of dehydrat-ing time remaining, the dehydrating time will count down in seconds. When no time is left, the word COOL will be displayed, accompanied by a series of beeps, followed by the fan being activated to cool the oven.

When the Instant Vortex Plus Air Fryer Oven is finished cooling, the word END will illuminate on the display, accompanied by another series of beeps.

Wearing your oven mitts, carefully open the glass air fryer door and remove the cauliflower crowns from the cooking chamber. Transfer to a bowl and let cool before serving. Garnish with fresh Italian parsley, if desired.

FUNCTION 7

ROTISSERIE

Unlike other countertop appliances or air fryers, large foods like a whole rotisserie chicken or beef roast are now possible at home thanks to the most popular feature of the Instant Vortex Plus Air Fryer Oven, the Rotisserie.

Yes, you can make a whole chicken or roast in the Instant Vortex Plus Air Fryer Oven two ways. The first, of course, is using the rotisserie to rotate the chicken or roast for even browning. But you can also set your chicken or roast on one of the cooking trays and turn it occasionally. In this chapter, we will be looking at how the rotisserie function works, which is also illustrated in the previous Roasting chapter.

How to Use the Rotisserie Function
Rotisserie Spit and Forks

After the meat, like a whole chicken or a beef roast, is seasoned and ready for roasting, you need to secure the food using the rotisserie spit and forks that are included with the Instant Vortex Plus Air Fryer Oven.

Begin by unscrewing the two set screws located on each fork. This can easily be done by hand.

Remove the forks from the long metal rod called the rotisserie spit.

Push the food, whether it's a whole chicken or beef roast, onto the rotisserie spit. Keep in mind that because the spit arm does not have a sharp point, it's helpful to guide the spit arm by first inserting a sharp rod or skewer into the meat before inserting the spit arm.

Slide the forks (screw side on top) onto both ends of the rotisserie spit, ensuring the fork prongs are inserted into the food to secure it in place. Then tighten each fork screw to secure the forks to the rotisserie spit.

Rotisserie Basket

For smaller, loose foods, like French fries or breaded shrimp, use the rotisserie basket, as illustrated in the Air Fryer chapter. The accompanying rotisserie lid has built-in spits at both ends, which will run along the guides in the cooking chamber.

Begin by adding the food inside the rotisserie basket, making sure not to overfill the basket. A good measure is to only fill your basket half full with food.

Secure the rotisserie basket lid on top by aligning the tab on the rotisserie basket with the notch in the lid. Turn the lid clockwise to "lock" it in place. A "lock-unlock" diagram on top of the lid will help you turn the lid in the proper direction.

Rotisserie Preparation

Whether you're using the rotisserie spit and forks or the rotisserie basket, both rotisserie accessories are installed and removed in the same way.

Before cooking, always make sure the drip pan is in place on the bottom of the cooking chamber before using the rotisserie function. A good kitchen practice is to line the drip pan with aluminum foil for easy cleanup.

Before preheating your Instant Vortex Plus Air Fryer Oven, always insert the rotisserie accessories and food first.

Rotisserie Catch Lever

This is the red lever you will find on the left-hand side after you open the glass air fryer door. Moving the lever to the right will allow the rotisserie catch to retract. Look inside the air fryer door as you move the lever to the right, and you will see a small black knob on the left that moves with the lever. This is the rotisserie catch that creates the space to receive the rotisserie spit from either the rotisserie spit and forks or the rotisserie basket.

Securing the Rotisserie

Holding the rotisserie catch lever to the right, slide the rotisserie spit along the guides in the cooking chamber. Use the rotisserie fetch tool that's included with the Instant Vortex Plus Air Fryer Oven to insert and remove the rotisserie spit after cooking.

Align the rotisserie spit of either accessory with the hole in the center of the rotisserie catch, then release the rotisserie catch lever to lock the spit arm firmly in place. You may have to wiggle the arm or rotate the basket a little so the left arm "locks" inside the rotisserie catch. You will hear a locking noise, confirming the rotisserie spit is locked in place. Wiggle the rotisserie spit to make sure it's held firmly in place on both sides of the cooking chamber.

Once the rotisserie food is secured in place, close the glass air fryer door.

Starting the Rotisserie

Select the AirFry or Roast function from the Control Panel display, depending on what you're cooking.

Next, select the desired cooking temperature by touching the temperature +/- control on the left side. Select the desired cooking time by touching the time +/- control on the right side.

When cooking begins, press the Rotate button to turn the rotisserie rotation on or off. It's good to have the rotation on when roasting such foods as whole chicken for a nice, even roast.

Then press Start.

Finishing the Rotisserie

When finished cooking, wear your oven mitts and carefully open the glass air fryer door. Use caution, because the door and accessories will be hot.

To release the rotisserie spit from either the rotisserie spit and forks or the rotisserie basket, insert the rotisserie fetch tool to "hook" the spit arms on each side. Now, carefully move the rotisserie catch lever to the right to release.

Slowly pull the rotisserie spit and forks or the rotisserie basket toward you, then release the rotisserie catch lever.

Carefully slide the spit arms back along the guides to remove the rotisserie accessory and food from the cooking chamber.

CARE AND CLEANING

Before cleaning your Instant Vortex Plus Air Fryer Oven, make sure the oven is unplugged and the appliance has cooled to room temperature.

Never use harsh chemical detergents, scouring pads, or abrasive powders on any of the parts or components of the Instant Vortex Plus Air Fryer Oven.

To clean, begin with the removable air fryer door. Always use a damp cloth to wipe the glass and allow to air dry completely before use.

To remove the door, simply open the door about forty-five degrees, hold the top of the door firmly, and gently pull up. The door will come unhinged, making for easy cleaning. Use a damp cloth or kitchen sponge with some soapy water, and *never* submerge the door in water or place inside the dishwasher. To reattach the door, angle the door at about forty-five degrees, hold the top of the door firmly, push down, and wiggle in place. The door should reattach as easily as it was removed.

For the rotisserie basket, a best practice is to clean the basket after each use. A kitchen brush and a little soapy water are all you need. To help with keeping the basket clean, use a nonstick cooking spray before adding the food. The basket is also dishwasher safe.

Like the rotisserie basket, the rotisserie spit and forks are dishwasher safe and should be disassembled from the oven and cleaned after each use.

The cooking trays and drip pan should also be cleaned after each use. Just use some soapy water and a kitchen sponge. Make sure all grease and food debris are removed from the Teflon-coated trays before use. All three pans are also dishwasher safe. For even easier cleanup, line the drip pan with aluminum foil before cooking.

With the cooking chamber, the chamber itself is not coated with any nonstick coating and should be cleaned after each use after the oven has cooled to room temperature. Always hand wash the chamber using a damp cloth or soft kitchen sponge. The heating element, chamber walls, and surrounding area should be cleaned of any grease or food debris. For stubborn grease and residue, you can use a commercial oven cleaner or a mixture of baking soda and vinegar. When applying, allow the cleaning agent to sit on the affected area for several minutes before attempting to clean.

To clean the outside of the Instant Vortex Plus Air Fryer Oven, wipe clean with a soft, damp cloth or soft kitchen sponge. Wipe dry to avoid streaking.

SAFETY FIRST

To avoid the risk of serious injury when using the Instant Vortex Plus Air Fryer Oven, please follow the following safety precautions:

Always use the Instant Vortex Plus Air Fryer Oven on a stable, level counter, table, or surface, and away from combustible material and external heat sources. Do not place on any kind of stovetop or in a heated oven.

Leave at least five inches around the oven and make sure not to place anything on top of the oven.

Do not block the hot air vent in the back of the appliance and never try and touch the vent during the cooking process.

Do not touch any of the oven's outer surfaces, which may be hot. Wear Instant Pot Mini Mitts or oven mitts to handle hot components or when opening and closing the glass air fryer door. Never put unprotected hands inside the oven until it has cooled to room temperature.

Always allow the oven to cool to room temperature before attempting to move the oven.

Never rinse the Instant Vortex Plus Air Fryer Oven under running water.

To protect against the risk of electrical shock, never immerse the power cord, plug, or the oven itself in water or other liquid. Also, never expose the power cord and plug to any hot surfaces or open flame, including a stovetop. Always keep the power cord and plug away from children and never drape the cord over the edge of a table or counter.

Never plug the power cord and plug from the Instant Vortex Plus Air Fryer Oven into an extension cord or use with power converters, adapters, or timer switches.

Never put liquid of any kind into the cooking chamber, including cooking oil, as the oven contains electrical components.

Do not overfill the cooking trays with food. Overfilling may cause the food to come in contact with the oven's heating elements, resulting in a possible fire or personal injury. Also, do not insert oversize foods and/or metal utensils into the cooking chamber and never place any combustible materials such as paper, plastic, or wood into the chamber.

In the case of burning or smoke, press Cancel and carefully unplug the appliance immediately. Wait for the smoke to stop before opening the glass air fryer door to inspect.

Children should never use the Instant Vortex Plus Air Fryer Oven without close supervision by an adult.

Do not leave the Instant Vortex Plus Air Fryer Oven unattended while in use.

When not using the Instant Vortex Plus Air Fryer Oven, the appliance should always be unplugged. To unplug, grasp the plug and slowly pull from the outlet. Never pull from the power cord.

Always inspect the Instant Vortex Plus Air Fryer Oven prior to use. Do not use the oven if the power cord or plug is damaged, or if the oven malfunctions, or is dropped or damaged.

Do not use any accessories or attachments that are not authorized by Instant Brands, which manufactures the Vortex Plus Air Fryer Oven. Some accessories or attachments not recommended by the manufacturer may cause a risk of injury due to fire or electrical shock.

Do not use the Instant Vortex Plus Air Fryer Oven outdoors.

Do not attempt to repair or modify the Instant Vortex Plus Air Fryer Oven and do not tamper with the safety mechanisms of the appliance.

ABOUT THE AUTHOR

James O. Fraioli is an accomplished cookbook author with a James Beard Award to his credit. He's published more than thirty-five celebrated culinary books, which have been featured on Food Network, *The Ellen DeGeneres Show*, and Martha Stewart Living Radio; and in *O: The Oprah Magazine*, *Vogue*, *Forbes*, the *Wall Street Journal*, and the *New York Times*. He's best known for teaming up with chefs, restaurants, mixologists, and industry professionals to showcase the best the culinary world has to offer. Prior to his successful culinary book publishing career, James served as a contributing writer and editor for dozens of food and wine magazines. He resides just outside Seattle, Washington. Visit him online at culinarybookcreations.com.

CONVERSION CHART

METRIC AND IMPERIAL CONVERSIONS
(These conversions are rounded for convenience)

Ingredient	Cups/Tablespoons/ Teaspoons	Ounces	Grams/Milliliters
Butter	1 cup/ 16 tablespoons/ 2 sticks	8 ounces	230 grams
Cheese, shredded	1 cup	4 ounces	110 grams
Cornstarch	1 tablespoon	0.3 ounce	8 grams
Cream cheese	1 tablespoon	0.5 ounce	14.5 grams
Flour, all-purpose	1 cup/1 tablespoon	4.5 ounces/0.3 ounce	125 grams/8 grams
Flour, whole wheat	1 cup	4 ounces	120 grams
Fruit, dried	1 cup	4 ounces	120 grams
Fruits or veggies, chopped	1 cup	5 to 7 ounces	145 to 200 grams
Fruits or veggies, puréed	1 cup	8.5 ounces	245 grams
Honey, maple syrup, or corn syrup	1 tablespoon	0.75 ounce	20 grams
Liquids: cream, milk, water, or juice	1 cup	8 fluid ounces	240 milliliters
Oats	1 cup	5.5 ounces	150 grams
Salt	1 teaspoon	0.2 ounces	6 grams
Spices: cinnamon, cloves, ginger, or nutmeg (ground)	1 teaspoon	0.2 ounce	5 milliliters
Sugar, brown, firmly packed	1 cup	7 ounces	200 grams
Sugar, white	1 cup/1 tablespoon	7 ounces/0.5 ounce	200 grams/12.5 grams
Vanilla extract	1 teaspoon	0.2 ounce	4 grams

INDEX

NOTES

··

··

··

··

··

··

··

··

··

··

··

··

··

NOTES

....

....

....

....

....

....

....

....

....

....

....

....

NOTES

....

....

....

....

....

....

....

....

....

....

....

....

....

NOTES

....

....

....

....

....

....

....

....

....

....

....

....

....

NOTES

....
....
....
....
....
....
....
....
....
....
....
....
....